A Cup of My Coffee 3
Lessons for Military Leaders

Scott H. Dearduff

Copyright © 2015 Scott H. Dearduff
Dearduff Consulting Agency, LLC
Peoria Arizona
Dearduffconsulting@gmail.com
All rights reserved.

Disclaimer: Although this book contains references to U.S. military services, specifically the United States Air Force, the thoughts, opinions, anecdotes, and lessons contained in this book belong to Dearduff Consulting Agency, LLC. There is no official endorsement of this book or the material within by any element of the Department of Defense, the U.S. Air Force, or any of the military units I was assigned to during my career. The use of the term Air Force is a simple reference and in no way is intended to imply official sanctioning by that military service. This book contains no classified information, and no references are made that would endanger military personnel or operations.

First Edition

ISBN-10: 1512241377
ISBN-13: 978-1512241372

DEDICATION

This book is dedicated to those who choose to lead men and women in the U.S. military during tough times. Your challenges are great, and you need all the tools you can get to manage your way through them. I hope this book provides some assistance in helping you accomplish your mission.

CONTENTS

1	The Mailbox Story	Pg #1
2	Stay in Your Lane	Pg #7
3	The Equipment Guy	Pg #13
4	Just Fix Trucks	Pg #19
5	Walk the Mile	Pg #25
6	A Cup of My Coffee	Pg #31
7	A Good Mirror	Pg #37
8	Improve the Foxhole	Pg #43
9	The Leadership Line	Pg #49
10	Courageous Leadership	Pg #55
	Glossary of Lessons	Pg #62
	Answer Key	Pg #64
	Appendix	Pg #65
	About the Author	Pg #106

ACKNOWLEDGMENTS

The stories in this book are a compilation of lessons learned over a long and challenging career. There are so many people to thank for helping me learn and grow…too many to list here. I'd like to specifically thank the following people who contributed directly to one or more of the stories in this book:

Robert D. Gaylor
Boudreaux Guidry
Chas H. Browning
R. Wayne Purser
Robin Rand
Gary L. North

And special thanks to those who reviewed and provided inputs on the contents of the book:

Mags Dearduff
Lefford Fate
Kirk Pontow
Kenneth Woodcock

INTRODUCTION

Military leadership has changed many times based on world wars and circumstances facing the nation. What remains the same is that military units need leaders. Troops need leaders. And even those in leadership positions need leaders above them to help guide them toward successful mission accomplishment. Without highly effective leadership, military units are destined to fail.

Being a military leader today requires more than just being the ranking person in the unit. You have to understand the mission, understand your troops, deal with their personal issues, and provide them with a stable, disciplined environment. Some would offer that you have to be kinder and gentler. I disagree. In fact, tough leadership is more important today than ever before. Modern troops are individualistic and want the freedom to make choices. They like their personal time and modern technology dominates their lives. You are not going to change those things, so why not embrace them.

A modern military leader has to be ready to incorporate new technology into their operation. If a leader insists on not using technology and tries to maintain the "old school" ways of doing things, they will soon find themselves becoming less relevant to the troops. Don't worry, they know you are older and have been around longer. They will think of you as old school no matter what you do, so hanging on to old ways is not always a positive approach.

Leaders have to motivate their troops. This does not always mean standing in front of them and being the loudest voice. This could mean being the person in the back of the formation because you gave someone else a chance to lead and take responsibility for the particular mission that you are on.

There is more than one way to lead in the military. I wish you luck in all of your leadership challenges and hope this book helps.

Throughout this book the term "troop" is used generically to refer to Soldiers, Sailors, Airmen and Marines

Dearduff

1
THE MAILBOX STORY

Back in my neighborhood there was one person who always got my attention. When I went past his home, I noticed several things right away. The grass in his yard was evenly cut and the edges of the yard were neatly trimmed. There were no leaves from the trees or loose trash laying on the yard. If his cars were in the driveway they were always clean and polished, appearing like they just came from the showroom floor. Even the windows on his house shined in the afternoon sun, never seeming to have any dirt or dust on them.

Being a curious young man, I decided one day that I would approach him and ask why these things were always as I had noticed. I arrived at his yard and introduced myself, then said; "Sir, can I ask you a question?" Without hesitation he replied; "Sure kid, go ahead."

I looked right at him with great curiosity and said; "Mister, why is your house and yard always kept so neat and your cars always so shiny?" He looked at me without much of an expression and simply said; "Because my name is on the mailbox."

Trying to make sure I heard him correctly, I replied; "Sir, I'm not sure I understand." He smiled at me and said; "Although we are neighbors, you don't really know me and before today we've hardly ever spoken. Even though we don't have a bond, you form an opinion of me based on what you see when you go by. You look at the end of the driveway and you see my name on the mailbox telling you that I live here."

I was not sure what he meant so I asked again; "Sir, I don't understand what your name on the mailbox has to do with this." He said; "I want you to form a good opinion of me. Therefore I make my house, yard, and cars look right in hopes that you will respect me because I take pride in the things that I have." I smiled and said; "Now I got it!"

Years later I became a leader in a large military organization with thousands of people working in dozens of divisions around the base. It was the largest responsibility I'd ever taken on. I knew that it would be hard to get to know each and every one of them, but it was essential that I set a good example and gain their respect during the few minutes of interaction that we would have together.

Our unit often hosted groups of local government and business leaders for a tour of the base. Every tour included a visit to the weapons storage area. Our Airmen demonstrated for the visitors how they built bombs that would go on our aircraft during combat operations.

It was an exciting time for most civilians--normally a once in a lifetime experience. Having seen this demonstration many times before, I used this time to visit with Airmen who were not directly involved. I walked down the line and thanked each one of them for their service and for the mission they performed in preparing our weapons.

As I got near the end of the line a young Airman shook my hand and looked me in the eye. It appeared he wanted to talk about something but was unsure if he should. He said; "Chief, can I ask you a question?" "Sure kid, go ahead" I told him. He said; "Chief, why do you always have shiny boots?" Looking back at him I said; "That's easy young man, because my name is on the mailbox."

He looked at me with the same look I had back in the neighborhood. He asked; "What do you mean?" Pulling him off to the side of the formation I explained the mailbox story to him from my childhood. Then I said; "You know you hardly know me as your command chief. You rarely get to see me out and around the organization because of the size and complexity of the place. And before today we've rarely spoken. But when you do get to see me you form an opinion based on what you see when I walk by."

And then I pointed to the left pocket on my shirt and said; "And my name is right here on the mailbox." I could tell he was taking this lesson in easier than I did as a young kid in the neighborhood, so I did not belabor the point. Continuing on I said, "I want you to form a positive impression of me and not a poor one. I want you to trust me so that if we deploy to combat together you will follow me into battle."

Motioning to my boots I said; "By shining my boots, keeping my uniform clean and pressed, and my hair neatly groomed, you remain confident that I take pride in everything that I do. You will believe that I take pride in all of my work, and that you can trust in my ability to lead you and the others when times are tough." With that he smiled, thanked me, and returned to the line with the others. The lesson had been passed on.

Several months later we repeated the base tour experience with another group of local dignitaries and took them out for the same demonstration. As always, there were Airmen standing to the side who were not involved in the event, so off I went to spend time with them.

As I worked my way down the line the second person encountered was that same young Airman from the previous visit. He stood there, tall and proud. His boots shining in the sun, uniform neatly pressed, and his shoulders drawn back. It was clear that he was a proud young man. We shook hands and smiled. I said to him; "Good to see your name on the mailbox." He said; "Good to see your name on your mailbox too, chief."

Reaching the end of the line, a supervisor from the section stopped me and said; "Chief, can you tell me that mailbox story?" I looked at him and said; "What story is that?" He smiled at me and said; "I don't know, but you told my Airman some story about a mailbox the last time you were here. And, ever since that day, he comes to work with his boots shined and his uniform is neatly pressed. His hair is always clean cut and he is neatly groomed." After a short hesitation he continued; "His records are up to date and when he completes his work, he volunteers for more. He takes pride in everything he does!"

I smiled and looked at the supervisor. I said; "My friend, you just told me the mailbox story." Turning to walk away, I glanced over at the proud young man at the front of the line and realized that he not only ingrained the mailbox story into his own life, but he impacted others through his actions. He clearly put his name on the mailbox!

THOUGHTS FOR SUCCESS:

Expectations for military leaders: Military units are being stripped of manpower authorizations and asked to continue meeting mission demands with fewer people. Budget uncertainty drives procurement decisions every year. These items add stress to the daily operations tempo of every military leader. But, you are expected to perform, produce, and provide solid leadership for your troops. While you are doing all those things, you also have to work on your own development and be involved in the community. How you handle yourself during all of this will determine how you are perceived as a leader. Nobody ever said that leadership was going to be easy.

Actions speak louder than words: How you act will be more important than what you say. Taking pride in those actions will increase your chance of success. You will lose credibility if you do not follow through with actions that match your words. You have to lead by action and ensure that you are not asking people to do things that you are not willing to do yourself.

Leadership demands high moral conduct: You can say all the right things, but if you act immorally, you will not be respected. Moral conduct is watched on and off duty. If you are acting foolish in your off time, and then posting it on social media for everyone to see, you will lose their respect. Your troops will form their opinion of you based on what they see posted on your social media accounts. A leader should not be "friends" with the troops on social sites. If you must engage in this fashion, keep it on one of the professional social media sites.

You are never off the leadership clock: By definition, a leader is a role model. You only have the choice of determining what kind of role model you will be.

The Lesson

Take pride in everything you do

Troops form an opinion based on what they see

A leader puts their name on the mailbox by:

- Displaying pride in personal appearance

- Developing trust with their troops

- Performing duties to the best of their ability

Benefits of using this lesson:

- Self-respect is contagious

- Troops follow a prideful leader

- Troops will trust their leader

2
STAY IN YOUR LANE

The day was long and the action was intense. A battle had been fought, and although it was only against a simulated enemy, our forces had overcome many obstacles and emerged victorious. Military units from all services are often tested on our ability to accomplish the wartime mission through a series of official tests and inspections. Undoubtedly, this one was the toughest we would face for many years.

During this particular battle my duty was to run the radio and telephone communications center that was responsible for the direction and control of all responding forces. At this time in my young career, I considered myself qualified beyond any of my peers and many of the supervisors with whom I worked. The worst part was that I often let it be known through my words and actions without realizing how I was coming across.

With the results of the inspection posted, it was clear that we had done well to defeat the simulated enemy. There were even comments about the expertise of the unit's "...command and control element," which I felt responsible for.

I was proud of my actions and accepted the praise with a great sense of pride. Everyone around me seemed pleased at my ability to handle this tough duty and they let it be known publicly. It was a great time for me and I could not have been more proud.

My confidence had grown so much that I got out in front of myself. Although it was good to have the confidence, I soon learned that I was crossing the line and had become cocky. There is a fine line between being confident and being cocky. It seemed I had reached new levels of cockiness.

A few days after the inspection was over I was visited on my post by a senior leader in my unit who had almost twenty years of service under his belt at the time. He sat with me quietly, watching me control the actions of the on duty forces.

His actions led me to believe that he was not paying me any attention and that I was in complete control. His duty was to manage the entire operation and his reputation was sound. Some of his predecessors led differently, often giving me free rein to run more than my share, and often times they sat back and let me run theirs. As the day progressed, he watched with more intensity and then finally spoke up.

The conversation began when he started by saying; "So you think you are pretty good at this controller business don't you?" I said; "Yes I do, and I proved it during the last inspection." Smiling back at me he said; "You think you have this all figured out don't you?" And again I replied; "Yes I do, and everyone seems to agree with me." He continued his line of questioning me by asking; "You think you are smart enough to do my job don't you?"

Even though I had 3 years of time in service, and he was a senior NCO, I said; "Yes, I think I can." In his own quiet, yet stern way, he looked at me and continued the conversation; "Well you are not." Momentarily stunned, I wanted to ask him what he meant by his comment, but before I could ask he said; "You're not as smart as me and you cannot do my job. There are just so many things you don't know at this point in your career and with your limited experiences. In fact, you are not even the best person we have assigned to do your job. You have a lot to learn and all the time in the world to learn it."

My leader was telling me that I was not good enough to be considered the best at my job. This was a tough thing to hear and I wanted to argue with him by defending my actions, but he continued; "When you decide to concentrate your efforts on the duty assignment I have given you and stop worrying about doing my job or others' jobs, you will begin the process of becoming an expert." He went on; "I call this staying in your lane."

He hesitated for a moment while I soaked in what he said. All the while I was thinking about all the praise I received from the inspection results and wondered why he would feel this way.

Before I could even ask a question he went on in his calm tone; "When you learn to stay in your lane and fully understand the skills required to do the job I have assigned you to do, people will respect your level of expertise and they will trust you more. Most importantly, when you have demonstrated that level of skill and ability, I will walk in here and promote you."

Now he really had my attention. I thought I was good at my job and that I could take on more. I wanted to progress and get promoted to have the additional responsibility. But it was becoming more and more apparent that my path to getting there was not the best way. He went on; "And once you learn to become an expert at that level, and handle the duties you are assigned, then I will walk in and promote you again." Simply put, he was telling me that I was hindering my progression by getting out of my lane. As much as I wanted to progress, there was little doubt in my mind that I wanted it to be done the right way. I was listening.

This was the feedback that I needed as a young professional before I ruined my own career. It was honest and direct feedback that was hard to take at first. But after considerable analysis, it really made sense.

Over the next few days I kept the information to myself. I did not speak to friends or colleagues. I became emotional every time I recounted the conversation. As difficult as it was, I needed to remind myself that his advice was sound, and would most likely lead to some level of success in my military career. I was determined to succeed, be good at what I was assigned to do, and make my family proud of my effort. There was only one thing to do and that was to make a positive change in my behavior, concentrate all of my effort on the job he assigned to me and become an expert.

This lesson paid great dividends during my NCO and senior NCO years. When I found myself getting outside of my lane, I would recount the lesson and bring myself back to reality. Staying in my lane helped me reach a high level of expertise and complete some difficult duty assignments.

The advice I received from my senior NCO about getting promoted by focusing on what I was assigned to do, worked out very well. Those promotions he talked about, they came along when I least expected them, because I was busy concentrating on being an expert at what I was tasked to do.

THOUGHTS FOR SUCCESS:

Know your position in the chain: Military leadership is often based on your position in the chain of command. If you desire to rise up the chain, start by becoming an expert at the level you have been assigned and work your way up as opportunities present themselves, in due time.

Be careful how fast you move up: If you are not an expert at your level when you are asked to move up, you will already be behind and you can expect to struggle. This will require you to work hard at developing yourself as a leader while continuing to build on your own professional growth and development.

Don't forget where you came from: Everything you learned as a junior enlisted member or junior officer helped you get to a leadership position. But you should not spend time talking about how you did things back in the day. The troops don't care about your "back in the day" stuff because they don't consider it relevant to their situation. Keep everything you have learned readily available to guide you in your actions, but ensure that all of your conversations and actions are focused on your leadership role and responsibility. People do not care what you did at your last base, post or ship. They only care about what you can do now.

Don't speak out on issues that are not in your lane: Keep your opinions close at hand until someone asks you for it. Be ready to share your thoughts when asked. Fellow military leaders are likely to accept your thoughts with openness when delivered in this manner. If you get out of your lane and speak openly about issues other leaders are trying to solve, they may be offended by the intrusion. Wait to be asked for your help unless it's a matter of safety or negatively impacts good order and discipline.

Mission success demands that everyone completes their own responsibilities and complement each other. By staying in your lane you will positively impact mission accomplishment.

The Lesson

Become an expert at your current job

Don't focus on what duty may be next

Military leaders who stay in their lane will:

- Increase their effectiveness in the assigned duties

- Grow and develop in the assigned role

- Open doors for greater responsibility

Benefits of using this lesson:

- Improved focus on assigned tasks

- Improved cooperation with other leaders

- Troops will support your effort and direction

3
THE EQUIPMENT GUY

Walking through the hallway one afternoon, my commanding officer was sharing his thoughts on an upcoming mission for our unit. We came across a young Airman in the hallway and the colonel stopped and engaged him, something that he always did. After a few short minutes of conversation, we moved on and continued the discussion.

We had just encountered one of the 386 people in our unit. I thought to myself there was no way that he knew everyone in the squadron or could remember their names. But during that brief encounter, the colonel spoke with that individual like they had known each other for years. I barely recognized the young man as a member of the unit and would have walked right past him in the local town if we were out of uniform. But the colonel knew him by name, and after a short greeting, asked the young man how his puppy dog was doing. I stood there in shock at what I witnessed.

How did the colonel know that this young man even had a puppy...or that it was sick? This level of knowledge about one of the Airmen was hard to grasp. Here was a man with huge responsibility for national security, but he knew the names of the masses who worked for him. I wanted to know more.

As we moved into his office to continue the talk, I stopped him and asked; "Sir, how is it that you knew that young man and how did you know he had a sick puppy dog?" He smiled and said; "Scotty, I make it my business to know them."

That seemed simple enough to me, but I was still confused. "What does that mean exactly?" I asked. He looked at me again and said; "Each member of the unit is important to the mission. They all have a part they play, a role they fill, no matter how large or small. The most junior person in the unit, with the most basic duties to complete, is an integral part of this team. If I don't know them, I can't ensure they knew how valuable they are to the team." It seemed to make sense to me now and we moved on.

Over many years and much travel, the lesson became a part of my personal philosophy. Traveling the battle fields of Iraq and Afghanistan, I would speak to large groups of Soldiers, Sailors, Airmen and Marines. Using this lesson I was able to motivate thousands by helping them understand that each and every one was important to the mission...important enough for me to get to know them.

<u>*My address to those audiences went like this:*</u>

Who remembers the Super Bowl in 2008? The game was between the New York Giants and the New England Patriots that included the most amazing catch ever in a big game.

With just minutes to go and the Giants trailing the Patriots, the Giants quarterback found himself scrambling for his life, and the life of the Giants if they were to win the game. He ducked, dodged, and finally ran his way free before launching a pass more than 40 yards down field to a heavily guarded receiver.

Miraculously, the receiver jumped between two defenders and grabbed the ball out of thin air with one hand, pinning the ball on the top of his helmet while falling sharply to the ground. He held on to that ball, creating a first down and a huge momentum swing for the Giants. They went on to score and eventually win the Super Bowl against the heavily favored Patriots.

There were many heroes that day for the Giants who were all celebrated on national television. As I watched the celebration, I wondered who the most important person on the Giants team was. Who was the person who contributed the most to the victory?

What do you all think? Who was the most important person on the Giants? (The most common responses were always like this): "It's the quarterback who threw the pass." "It was the receiver who caught the pass?" "No, it was the coach, the offensive line, the entire team!"

<u>Once I had all of their answers, I would continue</u>:

Some of you think the quarterback, the receiver or even the coach was the most important person on the Giants. But I think you have all overlooked one person whose performance for the team is crucial to every player on every play, and every aspect of the game. He has the most direct impact on individual performance. He makes sure everything is right even before the first whistle. Long before the players arrive and the training staff begins taping up ankles this guy is already on the scene setting up the gear. He makes sure the quarterback has the right length of cleat on his shoes to provide the best grip of the field. He even makes sure the footballs have the right amount of air so the kicker can perform at the crucial moment.

Yes, I'm talking about the equipment guy. He is the one who stands steady on the sideline waiting for a player to come out of the game with an equipment malfunction. Quickly assessing things, he gets the player back on the field. He performs on short notice and with exacting perfection. He finds ways to patch things up that are not replaceable.

When the game has ended, and the quarterback is announcing that he is going to some theme park to celebrate with his family, the equipment guy is already busy putting things away, and making sure they are ready for the next game.

The equipment guy hardly gets to celebrate the victory; he just goes back to work. The equipment guy is hardly thanked for his contribution, but he works harder than anyone on the team. The equipment guy may be the least athletic person of the entire staff, yet he possibly has the greatest impact on the game.

As a military leader I chose to know all of the equipment guys in my unit. Like the colonel taught me many years before, I made them my business. As a front line leader the guys on my team were welcomed, indoctrinated, trained, and cared for. I wanted to know their family situations, how many kids they had, and even when there were important days in their lives.

Sometimes the troops don't want you involved in their lives. Well, that's not OK with me. After moving into a new role as a leader, I once asked all of my direct reports to provide me with a personal data sheet to give me important information about themselves. One refused. I put his blank sheet on my desk and went about my business. Later he asked why I wanted that information. I told him it was not a big deal and if he wanted to leave it blank that was OK. But then I said; "Don't you have a young daughter, say, 3 or 4 years old?" He acknowledged that he did and she was 4. I told him, "I know how important a 5th birthday party is to a little girl and how big a deal that would be to have her dad there with her on that day. Wouldn't it be a shame if I did not know that her party was on a Saturday during the same week that we had major projects going on and I worked you late each night and into the weekend?" Before I could finish the conversation he grabbed the paper and filled it out.

There really is no secret to being a good military leader. But if there is one factor that can positively impact your results with the smallest investment, it would be taking time to know your people.

THOUGHTS FOR SUCCESS:

Dedicate time getting to know them: Don't just give them orders when they walk in and expect they will get right to work and produce high quality results. Troops want you to know something about them and they like their opinions to be acknowledged and considered. They also want to know things about you. While you should not get too personal with them, you should consider telling them about the things that are important to you. It will make you seem more human to them.

Commit time on your daily schedule: Every leader is busy and has many things to accomplish in any given duty day. By setting aside time to know your troops you will improve individual morale and increase productivity. While you are spending time with one troop, the others will be hard at work because they know you care about them as individuals who have lives outside of the military duty they swore to serve.

Tell me your story: When I first meet a new troop I simply ask them to tell me their story. Often the troop will say they don't have a story. When I convince them that everyone has a story, they start talking. After they get started they will share some interesting things about themselves. Everyone likes to tell their own story, they just need to know that you want to hear it. Once they do share things about themselves, you should lock that information away for future use. Asking them questions about the things that are important to them will go a long way in building your relationship.

Make the transition: Before you became a leader, you were a buddy, a friend, and a co-worker of the junior troops. But that changed when you were promoted and became a leader in your military service. Your leadership responsibility has priority over your friendships. You can still be friendly, but you have to lead first and gain their respect so they will follow. You cannot make everyone happy because you will be called upon to make decisions that are not popular.

The Lesson

Make it your business to know them

Spend time and check on them regularly

A military leader who spends time getting to know the equipment guy will:

- Make everyone feel equally important

- Build trust with their troops

- Remain approachable

Benefits of using this lesson:

- Troops work hard when they know you care

- Troops will bring problems to you

- Unit members feel inter-connected

4
JUST FIX TRUCKS

The heat of the Kuwaiti desert was nearly unbearable during the summer months. Operating in heat that exceeded 120 degrees made even the easy tasks of completing a mission difficult. But for those who were assigned to combat deployments, there were only two choices: complete the mission in that awful heat, or fail. For those of us in the armed forces, the second choice is not an option.

During one particularly hot September day in that Kuwaiti desert the travel itinerary included a visit to the transportation unit that held responsibility for all motor vehicles on the compound, around the clock, seven days a week.

This group consisted of vehicle operators, mechanics, supervisors and managers. They awaited my arrival and were all standing in formation as I entered the building. Quickly realizing that this formation was too formal and would hinder my ability to talk with the group and get the message across, I told the senior NCO in the unit to have them "fall out" of formation and gather around me.

It was hot, the building had no flow of air moving about, and the distinct smell of vehicle fluids filled the air.

Once the crowd of 40 or so got themselves situated in close proximity, I began talking about the things that were going on around the battlefields of Iraq and Afghanistan. It was always my intent to share the big picture of the combat zone, as each group was confined to their own battle space and their particular mission. During this portion of the war there was always bad news to share. Casualties were a daily reality. Sharing the stories and the names of those injured and killed in action always made the discussion somber, but also made it very meaningful.

Often I would pull the notebook out of my left pocket and share stories of the Airmen who made the ultimate sacrifice. The audience seemed to appreciate hearing their stories and knowing that we honor those we have lost. It was a great way to keep them attached to the front lines. Rarely were there dry eyes in the audience, including my own.

Next it was time to discuss my point of the trip. To ensure that each of them knew the mission and how they fit in. I had many options to choose from, but I looked around the group and found a young face in the crowd. This young man tried to avoid eye contact with me in fear of being called upon for some question or discussion. I walked directly over to him and introduced myself before asking his name.

Once he shared his name and his home town, I talked with him for a minute to ensure he was comfortable. The conversation went like this; "So, what is it that you do for the mission?" He looked at me shyly and said; "I just fix trucks."

I responded; "Is that important to the overall mission?" After hesitating for several seconds, he said; "I think so." The intensity of the conversation grew as I sought to get to the bottom of his reasoning by asking; "What do you mean, I think so?" He tried again by saying; "I think it is…and without hesitation he went on…You see that truck over there, that's the one I am working on. Once I get it fixed it will go back out on the flight line and will be used by the aircraft maintenance team to carry a tire for one of the refueling aircraft. If they cannot change that tire before it's supposed to fly tonight, the plane may not complete its mission."

I asked him for more information on this train of thought he was sharing. I said; "So what if that one plane does not complete its mission tonight?" Looking me directly in the eye, he said; "If that refueling plane does not fly tonight and have gas available for the fighter jets to keep flying, one of them may not be able to get their bombs on target on time."

Now we were getting somewhere, so I asked; "And what if they don't get their bombs on target, so what?" His confidence was now building with each response and the stress that was obvious before was now replaced with a sharp smile. He said; "If they don't get bombs on target in time, some Soldier, Sailor, Airman or Marine on the battlefield may die because they were not protected."

Before my arrival at his shop, this young man had no idea that I would call on him and no idea what I might ask if I did. But when he was put on the spot and asked if his job was important, he knew how important it was and he was able to explain it with conviction. His initial ability to relate "I just fix trucks" to bombs on target showed that he understood how he added value to the mission.

Rather than thinking tactically and only about the work he did to prepare that truck, he was able to see how his work was a critical part of supporting other people in their jobs. And by doing his job well, he contributed directly to completion of the mission.

It was the best answer I had ever received to that question. The NCOs in this unit seemed pleased that this young Airman was able to articulate his importance. I addressed the entire team again and told them how impressive it was that this Airman was able to think about his strategic impact. I applauded them for having a vision that went beyond turning wrenches and fixing trucks. I assured them that I had a high level of confidence in their ability to just fix trucks so that our battlefield warriors had every available resource ready to go each time they went out on the mission. It was also very clear to me that we had NCOs and officers in this unit who understood the need to connect Airmen to the mission.

By the end of the discussion everyone in the shop appeared to be motivated to get back to work. I was motivated to get to the next stop on my visit to see if there were more dedicated Airmen who understood the importance of their mission.

Throughout my career as a military leader there were many more opportunities to spend time helping troops understand this lesson. Sometimes the ones who could relate to the mission the best were the ones who were far from the center of attention. They dedicated themselves to knowing how important their job was to the overall mission, and could easily explain it to me when I visited.

I actually made a habit out of visiting those vehicle maintenance shops, but for more than the reasons in this lesson. You see, after my promotion to E-9, Chief Master Sergeant, I was given the opportunity to serve as a Command Chief. When I called and told my father, himself an Airman back in the 50s and 60s, what I was about do, he offered this advice; "Go see the guys in the motor pool." When I asked him why, he said; "Because when I was in the motor pool, you never came and saw me. The guys on my team never knew the chief, or never saw leaders, unless something was wrong. We all just wanted to feel like we added value to the mission, even though we were working nights and weekends in the motor pool, just fixing trucks."

THOUGHTS FOR SUCCESS:

Make a connection to the mission statement: Every military unit, at every level, has a mission statement. The higher the level of command, the broader that mission statement will be. Leaders must be able to explain how every troop adds value to the mission of your unit, the command and even the mission of your military service. There is always a bigger picture. But it takes every piece to make that picture complete.

Don't just recite the words: Make sure there is meaning to the words of the mission statement. Have them put it into their own words if they want. The real impact comes when they actually know what it means as they recite it. When they believe in the mission, and accept it as a guide to everything they do, you really have a good situation. Troops should be able to translate what they are going to do each day into the mission statement. This ability will help them understand that serving in the military is not like clocking in to a regular job, and that all jobs are important to the mission.

Incorporate the mission statement into regular activities: As a leader you have to find ways to use the mission statement in your everyday language. Relate what is going on at their level to the big picture. It will help them feel the connection to a higher calling.

The stakes are higher in combat: During peacetime or garrison operations, sometimes it may seem hard to relate front line troops to the mission statement. However, if you can do it then, before you go off to combat, it will be easier when you head into contingency operations. Missions in combat operations are normally much easier to understand and relate to because the stakes are higher. Make it your leadership objective to always be a mission focused person who does not wait until the stakes have raised to get serious.

Remember, even the guy whose job is to just fix trucks has an important role in putting the bombs on target. The better he can articulate that, the more focused he will be on the mission.

The Lesson

Everyone adds value to the mission

Help them relate to the mission statement

As a military leader you should:

- Bring clarity to the mission statement

- Focus troops on their particular duty position

- Explain why their contribution matters

Benefits of using this lesson:

- Troops feel good about their contribution

- Troops have individual buy-in for success

- Troops remain mission focused at all times

5
WALK THE MILE

For twenty-two years my work mainly consisted of security and law enforcement operations, with little exposure to other career paths or lines of business. Because of the extensive time I spent with nuclear security operations and presidential security, some considered me a real expert in those fields.

But with professional advancement came opportunities to lead people who had different professional backgrounds, and who cared little about my past. All they wanted to know was what I could do for them now that I had taken over as their command chief. In order to gain their confidence and build credibility, I had to act fast and show them I was serious about learning their jobs and how they contributed to the mission.

My new role included responsibility for aircraft maintenance, an area that was unfamiliar to me. There were hundreds of young men and women who spent their days working hard in very harsh conditions to keep the fleet of military fighter aircraft operational. It was obvious to everyone that my background lacked any maintenance experience, there was no disguising that.

In the early days of this two year tour of duty, one of the units offered to host me to "launch a jet" with them so that I could better understand what they did out on the flight line— the front line. They said it was one of the toughest things they did. I told them I would be honored and just needed to know what day and time.

They initially told me that I could launch a jet on Tuesday at ten fifteen and that I should arrive at nine forty-five. I looked at them with a puzzled gaze, I said; "I thought you told me this was a tough part of the operation?" They looked back just as puzzled and said that it's not only tough, it's one of the most critical operations that we do.

So I said; "Then it must take longer than 30 minutes for this to happen. I'm curious what time does the Airman I will be working with arrive?" Eventually they said, "Well he shows at six fifteen to get his tools, stand in a pre-mission briefing, and conduct a pre-walk of the area for foreign objects that may hinder the jet engine during the operation…but you don't have to worry about any of that, just show up at nine forty-five." I looked back and said firmly, "I will see you at six fifteen."

Arriving promptly at six fifteen in the morning it was already 95 degrees outside and somehow it's always warmer on the flight line. Upon arrival at the aircraft maintenance building, I noticed there was an E-4, senior Airman, standing at the door waiting to greet me. He introduced himself and said that we could get started right away, not wasting any time in case I had questions. Off to the tool barn we went.

We drug the 100 pound tool box out to the aircraft parking spot before we had to head for the briefing room. I fired questions at him as fast as he could answer them; and he handled them with ease. As we reached the briefing room the others were standing tall waiting for us.

We joined the formation and listened intently for assignments, safety messages and any other additional notes from the NCO in charge. When he was done, the NCO said "We have a special guest with us today…" But before he could say anything, I motioned to him and cut him off. Then I simply said, "I'm just another Airman standing in formation, waiting to go launch my jet, walking a mile in your shoes so that I experience what your troops do every day. Please do not treat me as a special guest, as it's important for me to know what it's like to take on this task of launching an aircraft." He smiled and moved on with the briefing.

The rest of the experience was fantastic. It was hot and the duties were demanding. Climbing under, on, and around the aircraft was extremely dangerous. Once that engine started, every move we made was critical, ensuring we prepared that aircraft for flight. Everything had to be perfect or we would be putting the pilot's life in jeopardy. And while I was learning about this critical task, I also learned everything I could about the Airman who was paired with me and the team he was assigned to.

By the end of that long day I learned what it was really like to be out on the flight line at 95 degrees performing a critical part of the mission. And I earned the respect of more than 200 people working on that team who undoubtedly passed that on to hundreds of others in the sister units. They seemed inspired by having a senior leader walking the mile with them on the front lines.

Throughout the next two years of that assignment, those same people lit up when I walked into a room. They showed new levels of motivation and talked about that jet launch as if it had just happened the day before, the impact was long lasting.

During the years that followed, I walked many miles in the boots of my troops. When time and the situation presented itself, I walked a few miles with my Soldier, Sailor and Marine battle buddies. The lessons I learned from being in joint operations paid great dividends for me when I attended professional military education courses with those fellow service members. There was a level of credibility in dealing with other service senior leaders when they knew I understood their missions, culture, and even their service terms. There was a high level of value placed on my inputs because I could speak their language.

The greatest benefit I found in walking those miles was the respect that I earned from the people I was standing next to. If they worked in the dining facility (chow hall), I went back there and cooked with them. If they swept the runway in a large vacuum truck, I rode with them. And when the heavy equipment operators offered me a chance to run a piece of heavy equipment, there was no hesitation.

On one particular occasion I was asked if I wanted to work a front end loader and help move some rocks from one area of the yard to another. Before the young NCO could finish the sentence, I was already stepping up into the cab and looking for my seatbelt. After a short explanation of the operating system, he jumped down and I was underway. I started moving rocks as instructed, and had a smile on my face the whole time. While I took it serious, I was really enjoying doing this kind of work. Then, I looked over at the NCO who gave me this opportunity and I could see the frustration on his face. I knew something was wrong, so I stopped my work and waved him over.

Once he climbed into the cab I asked him if I was doing something wrong. He held back, but eventually said, "Chief, you are not doing anything wrong, I'm just thinking that at the pace you are going, it's going to take me all day to get these rocks moved." We laughed, and I thanked him for the opportunity. I gave up my seat and he got back to work; at light speed compared to me.

It was the capper on this lesson that I needed. It's OK to walk those miles with your troops, just make sure that your presence and your actions do not get in the way of their success.

THOUGHTS FOR SUCCESS:

Earn their respect, don't demand it: Troops will speak to you respectfully in military formations and public settings. They will follow your orders and generally uphold the responsibility assigned to them. They do these things to survive in the unit. If you want them to buy in, to become fully supportive of you as their leader, one of the best things you can do is roll up your sleeves and dig in with them at their job. Troops have higher levels of respect for leaders who earn it rather than demand it.

Lose the sense of entitlement: Leaders must remain humble through their actions and show respect to the troops while walking a mile in their boots. Don't get caught up in the importance of your position and responsibility within the organization. Leaders who feel a sense of entitlement will lose track of the importance of spending time with their troops.

Pay attention to what you see and hear on the mile: While most troops will be cautious about telling you things in public, they will open up more when you are standing beside them working a mission objective. They will tell you how things are really going, what shortfalls they have in equipment, and they will often identify gaps in the processes they use every day. If they identify a real problem to you, there must be action and follow up. Once you have been told about a problem, it's now your problem to fix.

Don't over-react, just take action: If you are made aware of a safety issue, or something with life or death consequences, you have to take immediate action. Any other circumstances will require you to slow down and ask questions. While you gather details, ask for inputs and recommendations from the troops. It's quite possible the person with the best solution is the troop you are walking the mile with. Listen to what they have to offer and see if their solution is viable. If you have the authority to change a process and what they are offering makes sense, change it quickly and give them credit for it. This will bring a high level of value to the time you have spent walking the mile.

The Lesson

Experience what your troops do every day

Understand their challenges and issues

Walking the mile will help a leader:

- Identify gaps in processes

- Find solutions to problems that exist

- Remove barriers and obstacles to success

Benefits of using this lesson:

- Leaders gain better perspective

- Troops feel trusted and respected

- Troops understand you are concerned about them

6
A CUP OF MY COFFEE

Placed in charge of a major project to provide professional education and development to a large group of enlisted members, I began sending emails to request assistance from subject matter experts.

Times had changed and email was the newest tool we had for communications. We started to operate more on the email systems than any other communications medium, including telephones. Within days of sending the initial request, responses were coming in and people were committing to support the program that was being proposed. Most of the key players were on board...everyone seemed willing to help.

But there was one Chief Master Sergeant who seemed to be holding out and not responding to my email requests. He was a true expert in areas of this project that would lend a high degree of credibility to the team...we desperately needed his presence. Without him, the project could fall short of the objective.

A second email was sent with no response. Then a third email, same thing, no response. Finally after another week and a fourth email, a short response came through. It simply said, "Call my office." Picking up the phone immediately I spoke with a very polite secretary. She said, "The Chief would like to see you on Monday at 10 hundred hours."

It seemed strange to me that he wanted to meet in person; all I wanted was to get a commitment from him. It seemed there was little choice but to accept the meeting since we really needed him on this project. My hope was that he would have committed through email to supporting the effort like all the others did.

He clearly saw me walk into the secretary's area from his office when I arrived 10 minutes early, but he did not call me in. At exactly 10am he walked out, welcomed me, shook my hand with a firm grip and said, come and have a cup of my coffee.

He didn't ask if I wanted coffee, or if I even liked the stuff. But he brought me into the office and sat me down with a fresh cup of coffee. After a few minutes of personal chat about how I was doing and several drinks from the coffee mug on his desk, he said, "Now tell me what it is that you need from me for this project."

I said "All the details were contained in the email and I just need to know if you are on board for the project?" He looked at me and said, "Go ahead and tell me what it is you want from me."

I explained the details of the project, assuming that he did not understand the email. For the next 15 minutes we covered all of the details of the initial plan. We discussed the expected outcome and the potential obstacles to success. When I finished, he asked a few questions about the timing and the location for the project. Seeming satisfied, he said; "Good, now that is what I wanted to know about the project and I will be happy to assist."

With that he looked me right in the eye and said, "But, the next time that you want something from me, show me respect by meeting with me face to face over a cup of my coffee. Then, and only then, after you show me some level of respect and common courtesy, you can explain what you need from me."

Sitting upright in my chair I still did not get the point. I actually thought he was being a little too old school and that he should have just read the email and responded, time was critical after all. I must have looked confused sitting there waiting for some more information or a further explanation of his point. My confusion did not matter, because he seemed happy—and the most important piece of this endeavor was to gain his support.

Walking out of his office the message had not sunk in for me. What I missed was that he was trying to teach me the value of face to face meetings and showing respect before getting down to business.

In the years following this lesson, I figured out that electronic communications were important, but they were not the best means of conveying my messages. I quickly adapted this lesson and made every effort I could to meet fellow NCOs and officers face to face when we became acquainted or started a new project together.

Opportunities to exercise this lesson continued throughout my military career. On one particular occasion, my boss and I were working with a foreign military to complete a major renovation project of a runway that was critical to our mission support of the wars in Iraq and Afghanistan. We worked extensively with planners, developers, engineers, and a host of other critical people to formulate the plan for this project. Once everything was done, we requested a meeting with the senior military leader in the country. But to our surprise, the meeting request was denied. Instead, we were invited to join him at his personal residence.

When I received the news that we were invited for a recreational event rather than a business meeting it was not apparent to me what was about to happen. Then while traveling to the location, my boss reminded me about the lesson I had learned many years before. He simply said, "We need to go and show a little respect before we can get down to business." He was right and I knew it. The lesson was perfect for this situation and I only hoped that our effort would pay dividends and the project would be approved.

Several hours later, and five miles or so out to sea, we found ourselves fishing in the most beautiful water I had seen. Fish were landed continuously and the crew happily assisted each of us. During the excitement of the catch, my boss looked at the host country leader and simply asked, "Have you had a chance to look at that proposal yet?" To which the reply came, "No problem my friend, it is done."

On that occasion it was not a cup of coffee but a cup of tea followed by a fishing trip. The important factor was that we showed respect by joining him on a personal fishing venture. That effort resulted in gaining his support for a multi-million dollar project to improve our infrastructure and continue fighting two wars. Face to face meetings work, just go and have a cup of their coffee!

THOUGHTS FOR SUCCESS:

Increase effectiveness of important messages: Using the Face to Face (F2F) delivery of important messages and mission objectives will positively impact your ability to communicate with people. F2F presence allows you to read body language, determine passion, commitment, and understanding of the people you are meeting with. You will struggle to understand the factors listed above by using email communications only.

Gain support from key contributors: F2F meetings will prove to be the most effective way to gain support from others or help you find the right person for the job. Being F2F with someone when you are trying to gain their support for an idea makes it hard for them to ignore you. Sending an email to someone who works down the hallway instead of walking down there and talking with them will hinder your ability to gain their support.

Don't let distance become an obstacle: If geographic distance makes F2F meetings impossible, pick up the phone and speak to them directly. After that initial discussion you can follow up and share additional information through email. If this is going to be a long term project, go TDY to see them F2F early on to establish intent and show them the respect they deserve.

Gain respect by showing respect: It really is a two-way street. Those in your chain of command will appreciate that you took the time to prepare and meet. F2F meetings will allow them to ask additional questions and seek more information before they make critical decisions. Conversely, those under you in the chain of command will appreciate that you are seeking their ideas and opinions before you determine the next course of action on important matters.

Military leaders typically want to get things done without taking time for small talk. But, in this day and age, you have to take the time to show a level of respect or there may not be any business.

The Lesson

Show respect by meeting face to face

Communicate important messages in person

Leaders benefit from face to face meetings by:

- Creating mutual respect with others

- Communicating clear messages

- Improving collaboration on projects

Benefits of using this lesson:

- Tone of voice is understood

- Importance of the message is relayed

- Communication is verbal and non-verbal

7
A GOOD MIRROR

Driving through an entry control point on another extremely hot desert day in Iraq, the general and I would soon be escorting the Secretary of the Air Force and several high level dignitaries. During the dry run for this tour, I noticed an Airman standing post who appeared to have a full face beard. No problem right? Except that facial hair while in uniform is strictly forbidden unless specifically waived for medical reasons.

It was my responsibility to ensure that all standards were being met. When someone was granted a shaving waiver it had to be trimmed neatly, and maintained within length standards. This particular Airman stood out because his beard was thick and dark. In my opinion, an Airman who did not meet the standards and required a waiver was not the person I wanted representing our combat unit in front of the senior Air Force leader during his visit.

Shortly after passing this Airman, I notified his senior NCO that he should be switched out from that post before the Secretary came through. I moved on and never thought about it again.

Hours after the visit was over, the senior NCO I contacted earlier sent me an email with his thoughts on my decision. Reading his email with close scrutiny was essential to ensure my understanding of his intent. What immediately jumped off the page were sentences that were typed in all capital letters. Then the highlighted text stood out. Finally, the underlined and bold typed words jumped off the page at me, all of which appeared to have been done to express his passion for the message he was trying to present.

After reading it to the end the first time I sat back in my chair and took a deep breath. This email certainly required a second read to see if it gave the same impression before taking any action or responding in any way.

During a second review, something else came to my attention that I did not appreciate. It became apparent that he was yelling at me by the way he typed his email, in an effort to argue the point about his Airman not meeting standards.

A quick glance to the top of the page grabbed my attention as it showed that not only was he yelling at me on email, but he had copied several of his, and my, subordinates on this message. He was yelling at me on email in front of our subordinates.

After some time and careful thought, my email reply to all recipients looked like this: "…call my office." When he called I invited him over for some much needed feedback.

We exchanged brief pleasantries when he arrived. Then I informed him that I wanted to be a good mirror for him by providing feedback about the way he approached the situation from earlier in the day and help him reflect on his actions.

I started by saying; "I am going to give you some feedback about your handling of the situation today involving the Secretary and the method you used to convey your response. During this feedback I'd ask that you not respond to my inputs. I'd prefer you just listen. Feel free to write any notes you would like." He looked at me and said; "You mean you don't want me to ask questions or say anything?" I replied; "That's correct, just listen and take notes, not responding immediately to what I say, or defending your actions. When we are complete there is only one thing I want to hear from you and that is, thank you. After that you can depart and do what you want with my feedback. This is not personal, its business and it's intended to improve your performance." He acknowledged and we moved on.

I began; "It's apparent that you do not agree with my direction from earlier today. While I respect your desire to debate the issue, I do not appreciate the method you used to express it."

He tried to interrupt and explain himself. I stopped him, reminding him that he was told to just take notes and listen. Reluctantly he sat back. I continued; "By choosing to send me an email rather than call or see me in person, you did not give me the benefit of seeing your passion through non-verbal communication. I was left to interpret the tone of your message on my own. I've read each line of the email more than once to ensure that I truly understood your position. However, while reading it was hard to overlook the bold type, underlines, italics, highlights and capitalized words. Frankly, it came across as you yelling at me."

Again he tried to interject, so I motioned to him that I was not finished. As he sat back I noticed a change in his emotions. I continued with the conversation.

"Your email appeared to be an attack on my decision making. It appeared to be directly combative toward a lawful request that was made for the betterment of the entire unit. And it appeared to be an attack on me, all under the watchful eyes of the subordinates you copied on the email."

At that moment there was a silence in the room that needed no explanation. After a short pause I continued the conversation; "The action you took today in response to the situation was not proper and will not be tolerated. In the future, when you have something you would like to debate with me, take the time to contact me in person so that we can have the full discussion, face to face. I will listen to your thoughts and consider your request or actions. If you cannot get to me personally, reach me by phone and at least give me the benefit of hearing your voice."

He tried hard to hold back, but could not contain himself, he needed to speak. Before he could get words out, I finished my thoughts; "At this time I would just like you to say thanks and depart. Please consider the feedback I have given you and if there is a need for more discussion, we can sit down later."

As he got to the door he turned, looked back at me and said; "Thank you, that is the first time in my entire career that anyone has given me real honest and direct feedback. Thank you."

Providing feedback in this honest and direct way made him reflect and examine his actions, just like looking into a mirror. The intent was immediate and sustained improvement in his actions. Throughout the next six months he was seen leading his team with passion. There was never another situation of this nature and his every action in leading his team was positive.

People did not always like receiving honest and direct feedback. Sometimes they took it personal and it impacted them in negative ways. What they did not understand was that in combat, like in many other daily military operations, there is no time for debate over poor performance. Things have to be done correctly and timely. Otherwise, there could be mission failure.

THOUGHTS FOR SUCCESS:

Control the discussion: Giving honest and direct feedback to troops allows you to remain professional and in control of the discussion. This method offers a non-controversial way to provide feedback intended to create a positive change in behavior. Using this method is most effective in situations when performance is unacceptable. We used to call this wall-to-wall counseling…we don't use those words anymore.

Allow them to focus on your words: The troop receiving feedback in this format will focus on what you are saying. They will not spend time formulating their response when they should be listening. If you leave the door open for discussion, they will likely miss the real intent of the feedback because they are busy preparing their response while you are talking.

Feedback is not a personal attack: Do not allow a feedback situation on performance to become a personal matter. If you allow this to become personal, you may react harshly during the session and say things out of emotion rather than reason and logic. Your troop will not learn from this feedback, and the working relationship could be damaged for the long term.

Seek feedback for yourself: As a leader you will give plenty of feedback. You should also receive honest and direct feedback from your boss or a trusted mentor. Your mentor can provide you with sound advice on how to navigate through tough times as a leader. You can also get, and should seek feedback from your troops. If they feel empowered to offer you feedback in your direction, they will help you improve on your performance. If you find yourself operating without getting any feedback on your actions, go find a good mirror and ask for some.

Don't become so consumed with mirrors that you never pass by one. Some leaders seek feedback from everyone they encounter. People who seek that much feedback are normally insecure and need reassurance.

The Lesson

Provide honest and direct feedback

Maintain professionalism, leave emotions out

Feedback to your troops will help them:

- Understand the impact of their actions

- Remain accountable for their actions

- Know and understand your expectations

Benefits of using this lesson:

- Troops will focus on your words

- Feedback is clearly articulated

- Troops will respect your inputs

8
IMPROVE THE FOXHOLE

Following the terrorist attacks on America in September 2001, military members knew that our lives would never be the same. We needed to prepare ourselves for the challenges that were in front of us. There were pending deployments away from our families, and the challenges that come with operating in foreign lands.

Heading into the first deployment it was easy to have a plan, a set of ideas that should work, and high levels of enthusiasm to make it all happen. No challenge too tough. It was my time to make a difference in combat for my nation.

We hit the ground running and dug in fast to figure out what needed to be done. We realized that our location lacked some necessary physical security barriers at the perimeter that were within our capability and we got to work putting them in place.

Immediately some of the members of my team spoke out and thought we were re-inventing the wheel. "Why not leave it the way we found it," some would say. While others commented " Why are we always working so hard to improve things when we know the next team behind us will just change everything once we are gone?"

Late one hot afternoon, as we were placing a line of concertina wire out on the open desert floor it became clear to me that what we were doing was improving our foxhole. We had to improve it in order to keep the enemy out and allow our unit to accomplish the job of flying combat missions. We had to protect our flanks and all avenues of approach.

As our deployment began, the base itself was growing in size and population, and the additional traffic would increase the possibility that enemy forces could approach and breach the perimeter. There was no time for relaxation or complacency during this tour of duty.

While we continued working, one of the guys asked why we were trying so hard to improve things when the team before us had not. I told him that it was important for us to make these improvements now because things change with time and circumstances. I reminded him that they had a different set of challenges and we should not focus on what they did not do, but rather on what we needed to do.

He looked at me with confusion, so I explained to him again that we don't know what it was like for them in their time or what other priorities they had to deal with. I told him that it's quite possible they wanted to lay this perimeter line out but never got to it because they were building up the tent city that we enjoy each night once our mission is complete. This explanation seemed to make sense and he and the others went back to work.

I thought long and hard about the theory and how I could ingrain it in myself, and then share it with others to make it all worthwhile. As a fan of military history I knew that in World War II American troops spent days on end sitting in foxholes along the front line of the battlefield. Everyone understood the term foxhole, so I decided to incorporate what we were doing.

The phrase "Improve the Foxhole" became our mantra. We decided that we would work hard each day to make our location better for the next team or at the very least, leave it better than we found it. The team was taught that no matter what we found or what the conditions were when we started a new mission, we would not complain. It was clear that we did not have the same set of circumstances that our predecessors had and therefore we should not spend time worrying about it. We definitely did not need to take time to complain about it.

It was natural for troops to complain while they were working hard in the combat zone. Some days the work did not seem to make sense. They felt like the people before them didn't get anything done. When those comments were heard, I would immediately stop them in their tracks. This conversation seemed to repeat itself more often than I cared to hear. Each time I would tell the person complaining that we were not here with them and do not know their circumstances, so "Let's just improve the foxhole and move on."

A year after that first deployment, the same team was sent to Baghdad International Airport to maintain security of the most dangerous airport in the world. Each night brought on a series of attacks from enemy ground weapons, rockets and mortars. Rarely a night went by without a barrage of outgoing artillery placed around the perimeter. It was an extremely difficult environment.

Every night there were wounded warriors brought into the hospital for critical medical care. This mission would possibly be the toughest one we would ever face. It would have been easy to sit back and accept the status quo, not making any changes because we needed our rest by day, preparing for the attacks of the evening.

Instead, working 20 hours a day was the norm. The enemy always seemed to stop attacking between 2am and the late afternoon, so this was our time to handle improvements. A team of security specialists was scheduled for daily repairs to the fence line and entry points. It was the safest time for them to operate heavy machinery and the least likely time for the enemy to attack.

We produced a log of the things that needed our attention for immediate improvement. Most of the work consisted of placing barriers, wires, and obstacles to secure the perimeter. They each worked hard to improve the foxhole and they took personal responsibility for it.

Over time they had so ingrained this lesson that I no longer needed to remind them why we were working hard to improve things. The entire team challenged the status quo without prompting. They looked for ways to innovate our protection scheme on the battlefield. The lesson was completely effective. We made it our mission to leave things better than we found them.

Improving the foxhole is a great way to take a unit from bad habits to positive action. From poor performing to top performing. And in many cases throughout my years as a leader, there were opportunities to take over teams that needed to improve. Each time a new challenge started, we looked for ways to improve the foxhole. There was no focus on the past, and no complaining about the previous leadership. We just got down to business and starting making improvements where they needed to be made.

Military teams and entire units that work together based on positive actions, innovation, and challenging the status quo are highly successful at completing tough missions. As a leader, you should make it your mission to use this lesson and help the team reach their goals.

THOUGHTS FOR SUCCESS:

Don't break things that work: You may inherit a high performing team and they don't need to change the way they operate. If that is the case, encourage positive behavior and find other ways to improve the foxhole by challenging them to develop new ideas. Encourage the troops to offer suggestions and bring new ideas to the discussion. Your new ideas will be better received using this method. Above all else, commend the positive things that are going on and encourage more of the same.

Develop credibility before making changes: Leaders often have to take over new teams or entire units. When this happens, do not jump right in and start changing things, unless they are hard broke and that is part of your orders going in. In most new situations, you should go in and look around, evaluate the current situation, and ask some questions. After giving that some time, you can determine what is going well and what needs to change. Being a new leader in an organization does not give you instant credibility with people to make sweeping changes.

Review past performance: Before you decide what needs to change, take the opportunity to review inspection reports and detailed after action reviews from operations, training, and combat missions. These reports give a clear picture of the team's performance under pressure. Evaluate the discipline of the people in the unit and have discussions with them about the environment. Whatever you do, refrain from making comments about how bad things were and how you are going to fix everything.

Change is not easy for people to accept: Helping troops understand the need for change is your responsibility. If they say, "That's how we have always done that," you need to look real hard at challenging that action or process.

The Lesson

Leave it better than you found it

Never settle for the status quo

Leaders improve the foxhole by:

- Focusing on constant improvement

- Eliminating focus on the past

- Creating an environment of innovation

Benefits of using this lesson:

- Troops have pride of ownership for work

- Troops work to improve the unit

- Complaining decreases

9
THE LEADERSHIP LINE

The mission for the day was to travel out to several sites in Kuwait and conduct town hall meetings with deployed Airmen. After a quick breakfast and an hour ride on a very dangerous highway, we arrived at our first destination, an international airport where critical cargo moved into and out of Iraq.

During the town hall I planned to share the latest leadership messages and answer questions about what was going on around the rest of the combat zone. Shortly after arrival the senior NCO for the unit informed me that we would have to interrupt the town hall to perform an honor cordon when they were notified by the mortuary team. I agreed, and told him that it would be my highest honor to join them in the effort. An honor cordon was formed any time we performed a dignified transfer of human remains for those killed on the battlefield.

Walking through the passenger terminal I noticed a senior NCO standing off to the side in the waiting area. I walked over and spoke to him and asked if he was OK. He showed obvious signs of stress which could have meant he had been awake for some time while traveling. It could also mean he was stressed because something was wrong. I could not figure it out and he was not sharing.

Our town hall was interrupted for the dignified transfer. As we walked toward the flight line, it all came together. The Fallen Airman we would be honoring was the Explosive Ordnance Disposal (EOD) specialist who was reported as killed in action the day before. And the senior NCO I encountered was his escort.

More than 200 Airmen marched in formation toward the waiting aircraft. Once there, they formed two lines, facing inward and remaining silent. As the white transport vehicle approached carrying the fallen warrior, a booming voice sounded, "Detail, Attention!" In unison the formation snapped to attention. That was followed by "Present, Arms." Right arms rose slowly to render honors to the Fallen.

As the flag covered casket passed, tears rolled down many of the faces…faces of those who never knew the man inside. Minutes later a chaplain administered a final prayer with a group of ten of us standing nearby, including his escort. Solemnly, we all rendered a final salute and wished our warrior and his escort Godspeed and a safe journey home on the Angel Flight.

We reformed the group to complete the town hall discussion. Once complete, we headed back to the passenger terminal, where much to our surprise, stood the fallen warrior's escort. Within seconds we learned that he had been removed from the plane because of a technicality with his paperwork and that he was told the policy would not allow him to accompany the fallen warrior home. He was devastated…I was furious. There had to be an exception to policy for a situation like this, and I was determined to find it.

The escort desperately wanted to be on that plane and be the first one to meet the family on arrival. This situation was completely unacceptable…nowhere near normal. However, situations like this do not always go the way they are planned and sometimes there are deviations…this deviation needed to be dealt with fast.

A Cup of My Coffee 3

The rules that govern movement of remains was not crystal clear and nobody seemed to be able to explain them to me. I knew we had to act fast and figure out who the exception to policy authority was for this matter.

Within a few seconds, I approached the civilian in charge of the airfield and demanded the plane stop where it was and give us a minute to figure out what was wrong with the paperwork. He said that he did not have that authority, and he did not believe that I did either. I explained my position to him and that my boss was responsible for all aircraft movement in theater, so I needed some time to get his approval. Phone calls were made to the headquarters for the Central Command area of operations.

At one point, I was talking to the headquarters by phone, the civilian running the passenger terminal, the Army Sergeant who controlled paperwork, and several people who were with me at the time.

As we continued to work for an exception to policy, I directed someone to take the fallen warrior's escort in a vehicle and drive out to the location of the aircraft and to "…park in front of it if you have to." As I gave this direction, we were notified that the aircraft was already on the runway, cleared for takeoff. I was not done, and had to continue this effort to get him back on that plane.

Completing the phone call to the headquarters I slammed the phone down and instructed the civilian to direct the plane back to the parking spot and to take on this passenger. Reluctantly, he took my direction and requested the plane to return and park. He told me that he was not happy about it and that this would probably come back to haunt me. At that moment, I was willing to accept whatever punishment came my way, because what I was doing was absolutely the right thing to do.

Just then, the Army Sergeant who was responsible for this program returned to the passenger terminal and said that his team had made a mistake and the escort was actually authorized to be on that plane under a certain exception in cases like this. I threw the paperwork down on the counter for the civilian and headed out of the terminal without saying a word or waiting to hear what the exception actually was.

Arriving at the plane a few minutes later, I told the escort that things were worked out and that he was getting back on that plane and taking his battle buddy home to his family.

Words were not necessary. As he started to board the plane he simply turned and grabbed me in a battle hug. He looked me in the eye and said thanks, then walked onto the stairs of the plane. At the top of the stairs he turned and waved, and I believe I could see a sense of relief on his face, as he was going to be able to fulfill the highest duty a combat warrior can complete.

During that entire event, I had many things to consider. Nothing was black and white, and nothing was resting easily on the leadership line. The unusual exception to policy that I was asking for put me in a position of taking a huge risk. If I had been wrong, and he was not legitimately supposed to be on the plane, I could have been held accountable for my actions. I knew the possible circumstances, and considered all of the factors. I knew the risk was worth taking since this situation needed to be rectified. That escort needed to be on the plane with his fallen warrior. It was not a clear cut situation, but being willing to work outside the leadership line ensured the right thing was done.

Weeks after this event took place, the escort official shared an email story with the entire EOD community. He shared that his journey was filled with obstacles, but they were all overcome by leaders who knew how to get things done outside the line when things were not clear.

THOUGHTS FOR SUCCESS:

Operating on the leadership line: Military leaders who operate strictly based on the black and white written rules are working on the leadership line. This is a conservative way to operate and you can be successful using this method during normal day to day operations in garrison. However, if this is the only way you are comfortable making decisions, you are going to struggle during combat operations and other times that require critical thinking.

Understand the exceptions: Leaders who know where the line is, but consider the normal exceptions to policy (known) and abnormal exceptions to the policy (unknown), are seen as risk takers who are willing to make decisions once they know all of the factors. They know the rules and do not violate them, but they also look for areas that allow exceptions. Leaders who are comfortable working outside the line are often seen as problem solvers by their troops.

Accepting risk is part of being a leader: Leaders who work only on the line rarely take risks and often frustrate their troops. You have to know the rules, but consider the other options available. Determine what can be done when an exception to policy is in order. Seek information that is outside of the leadership line to help you make informed decisions in those cases and be willing to take on some risk. Don't just make decisions aimlessly, as those will get you into trouble and you will be held accountable. People are inspired by risk taking leaders and follow them with a higher degree of loyalty.

Understand the consequences: You have to know where the line is. Then, consider the exceptions to policy and decide if you can accept the risk of making a decision outside of the leadership line. It will be important to understand the full consequences of your actions. You should be confident in your decision because you will own it, and you are accountable for the outcome. If the decision turns out to be a bad one, you will be responsible for whatever happens.

The Lesson

Always consider exceptions to policy

Follow the rules and willingly take risk

A leader can work outside the lines if they;

- Understand all factors before deciding

- Articulate the reason for the decision

- Remain accountable for the decision

Benefits of using this lesson:

- Increased confidence in your decisions

- Available exceptions are considered

- Troops appreciate and follow bold leaders

10
COURAGEOUS LEADERSHIP

The weather was unusually warm on that October afternoon on the dangerous streets of Baghdad, Iraq. Regardless of the conditions, a group of Security Forces Airmen went headlong into their mission of training Iraqi Policemen.

A team of 13 Airmen, each with a specific role to play in the proper execution of the day's mission was quietly forming in the compound. As they prepared their gear, discussed procedures, and rehearsed their intended actions on contact, nobody knew what circumstances were in front of them or what challenges they would face.

For one young Security Force Airman, it would be his last mission. He was assigned as the heavy machine gunner, posted in the turret of an armored Humvee. At this time in the war, this was considered the most vulnerable position because of the exposure it created for the person. The gunner sat at the top of the vehicle with their body exposed on three sides. They were the first to see, and normally the first one exposed to enemy fire. It was a difficult position at best.

This particular Airman often volunteered for this role as he did not like having his friends and co-workers exposed to the extra danger. Today's challenge included supporting the Iraqi

Police after locals found an Improvised Explosive Device (IED) on the streets. The team responded to handle the situation just as they had many times before.

Immediately after arriving on scene, the brave young man rose from the turret of his vehicle in an attempt to stop women and children from entering the area. Within the first minute after arrival, he was shot and killed instantly when a sniper's bullet struck its intended target.

The team had no idea they were set up for this attack. The only thought on their minds was to depart the kill zone and hope to reach medical care in time to save their teammate.

Sadly, before they could make much progress at all, the team leader came to the realization that he had lost one of his men. A helicopter arrived and rapidly flew this injured warrior away to the combat surgical hospital, but it was too late. The team was in shock as they headed back to the camp. This was a tragic day for the team, the entire unit, and all of us in Iraq at the time.

One of the toughest duties a military leader is tasked with is facing tragedy in situations like this. A colonel with nearly 30 years in the Air Force and his senior enlisted advisor, a chief master sergeant, sped toward Baghdad to be with the unit as they dealt with the tragedy.

With the honor cordon formed and the dignified transfer ceremony complete, this Fallen Airmen departed for the trip home on his Angel flight. The other members of his unit returned to their compound and contemplated the long day and all that had taken place.

They sat around with long faces, covered in dirt, blood and tears. The emotions they held in all day were now letting go. As the night lingered on, the colonel and his chief went around person to person checking to see how they were coping. Along this path, they came across a young man who seemed to be taking the tragedy extremely hard. He looked at the colonel and simply asked; "What do we do now, what's next?"

At that moment in time, the colonel found himself at a fork in the leadership journey we refer to as a "Courageous Leadership" moment. He had two choices on how to handle this situation, each with their own set of outcomes.

Without hesitation, the steely eyed colonel looked that young man in the eye and said; "I'll tell you what now. Tonight we sit together and mourn the loss of our friend and fellow Airman. We laugh, we cry, we think about all the good times and bad."

He took a deep breath, then continued; "But what's next is tomorrow. For tomorrow we will mount up this team and go back out on the mission in the same streets of Baghdad." He paused for a few seconds and then said, "Because if it was worth our teammate giving his life for today, it's worth you and me doing it again tomorrow. So in his honor, we will go back out on the mission and complete it to the best of our ability."

The young Airman stood tall and thanked the colonel. He said, "Sir, thanks, that is exactly what I needed to hear." The colonel's ability to make the tough decision to get the team back on the mission during this difficult time added significantly to their motivation level.

The following day the team prepared their gear and cleaned their weapons in anticipation of the next mission. Their courage was tested, but with the reassurance from a courageous leader, they were ready to go back and face the same challenges as the previous day. The colonel and the chief were standing next to them, preparing for the same mission and the same danger.

My time in combat presented many other opportunities to witness courageous leadership in action. Following tragic events there were always difficult decisions to be made which were not popular and were not easily accepted by the masses. As a leader I had to ensure the courageous decision was made regardless of the personal feelings that may be impacted. It was my job, along with the other leaders of the unit to be strong in our conviction, know the circumstances or our actions, be willing to make decisions, and stand behind them.

Unfortunately not every situation in combat was handled properly or courageously. When leaders handled things poorly or took the easy road, there were always negative consequences. Troop morale was negatively impacted and mission objectives were not always met.

When a leader in one of my units made a poor decision during a crisis situation or during difficult times, I tried to spend time with them in hopes of controlling the damage. On more than one occasion poor decisions under crisis caused the death of troops under the command of those leaders. There is no way to recover from a tragedy that was driven by a poor decision. It was crucial, and will always be crucial in military operations, for leaders to think, plan, and act with courage to ensure they add to the success of the unit and their troops.

THOUGHTS FOR SUCCESS:

Explain yourself when time permits: Troops appreciate leaders who make decisions and stand behind them. And they like knowing that you will explain your decisions when time permits, so they understand your reasoning. But they do not expect you to explain yourself during a crisis situation. When there are bullets or blood, nobody will question your orders. Troops will act fast and efficient in order to eliminate the threat or control the chaos.

Choose the tough route over the easy way out: If you choose to take the easy route when you hit the fork in the leadership decision road your troops will lose confidence in you. Your commander may also lose confidence in you and that could damage your relationship. It may be difficult to make the tough decision, but it will be critical to ensure the success of the mission.

Compartmentalize your emotions: While leaders are people and have emotions, you have to learn to control those during difficult times. The troops are counting on you to be strong when they are weak. They are looking to you for confidence and strength when they are struggling. You will have a chance to deal with your emotions later, in private or with a trusted colleague. If there is a death in the unit, or some other tragic event, a leader will be expected to take the stage and be strong in delivering a message. The strength of that message will help many of your troops get through those difficult times. You are allowed to show some raw emotion, but it cannot overtake your ability to be the strength they need.

Courage is not guaranteed: Just because you are a leader does not mean that you are automatically courageous. It also does not mean that you will act courageously when the situation dictates. However, everyone has some level of courage in them, and have the ability to exercise it during difficult times. The more difficult things you deal with as a leader, the more comfortable you will become making courageous leadership decisions.

The Lesson

Make decisions during difficult times

Face difficulty with courage

A leader can display courageous leadership:

- When faced with tough decisions

- When faced with difficult circumstances

- To make unpopular decisions

Benefits of using this lesson:

- Emotions are kept in check

- Troops will follow with courage

- Troops will perform with confidence

A Cup of My Coffee 3

GLOSSARY OF THE LESSONS

THE MAILBOX STORY
Take pride in everything you do

STAY IN YOUR LANE
Become an expert at your current job

THE EQUIPMENT GUY
Make it your business to know them

JUST FIX TRUCKS
Everyone adds value to the mission

WALK THE MILE
Experience what your troops do every day

GLOSSARY OF THE LESSONS

A CUP OF MY COFFEE
Show respect by meeting face to face

A GOOD MIRROR
Provide honest and direct feedback

IMPROVE THE FOXHOLE
Leave it better than you found it

THE LEADERSHIP LINE
Always consider exceptions to policy

COURAGEOUS LEADERSHIP
Make decisions during difficult times

ANSWER KEY

If you are looking to this page of information for the answers to the leadership challenges that you will be faced with, you may have missed a major point in the understanding of leadership.

There are few answers in the book, any book, about how to handle leadership situations. Most leadership situations are not clear cut and require understanding and evaluation before deciding how to act.

In leadership you will find that no two situations are exactly alike. Leaders must make decisions based on their judgment, training and experience.

Judgment is your ability to decide based on the factors, conditions, and expected outcomes.

Training is gained over many years and through many sources.

Experience can only be gained by your direct involvement in situations.

APPENDIX

Now that you have read the lessons contained in the book, it's time to put yourself to the test by answering the questions in this workbook.

If this is being completed in a facilitated course, the instructor will lead you through each chapter. However, if you are doing this through self-study, you can go at your own pace. And while I recommend that you start with chapter 1 and work your way through each one, there really is no specific order that these lessons have to be discussed and your actions analyzed. In fact, you can pick the chapter that excites you the most and start there.

The real test of this leadership study will be for you to take a deep and honest look at yourself, answer the questions to the best of your ability based on how you are performing now, versus how you see yourself performing in the future. Be brutally honest, and you will see the benefits later when you find ways to improve your leadership performance. You should not expect to have all the right answers to every question.

By the end of this workbook you will be able to identify areas for improvement in your capabilities, actions, or attitude toward leadership situations. Be willing to make some commitments to improving in those areas. After you write down those commitments, check back on them often.

Allow yourself to be vulnerable when answering these questions. While you are discussing these lessons, continue to ask yourself if you love being a leader. Ask tough questions like; do I have the passion that it takes to lead people in all types of situations? Can I display that passion without making everything about emotions?

Good luck on this portion of the journey, and remember, be honest with yourself.

Lesson Reminder

Take pride in everything you do

Your name is always on the mailbox as a military leader. If you take and show pride in everything you do, people will see that you take pride and they will follow you with confidence. From dress and appearance to customs and courtesies, troops will constantly watch and evaluate everything that you do.

They form an opinion of you that can change in an instant if your actions are not consistent with your normal behavior. Consistency will help people form a solid opinion of you.

- What is the most important thing you took from this lesson?

- How do you display your name on the mailbox now?

- How do you think troops perceive you?

- How do your peers perceive you?

- How do senior officers/NCOs perceive you?

- What can you do to enhance perceptions?

List the items you will commit to in order to put your name on the mailbox:

1)

2)

3)

When will I have these items complete?

Who will hold me accountable for these actions?

What are the consequences of not doing these items?

FINAL THOUGHTS:

People say that you should not judge a book by the cover. I agree, but if the cover looks unappealing, I probably will not read the book. Therefore, if your name is not on the mailbox in a positive way, I may not follow you. If I am obligated to follow you because of your position in the chain of command, I will not have a high level of confidence in you.

Manage resources and lead people. Simple as that. Do not try to manage troops the way you manage supplies, budgets, or physical resources. Troops like to work for leaders who care about them. Before you can care about them, you have to care about yourself and the things you are responsible for. Be proud of who you are and it will reflect in your actions.

Start off each day by thinking about how you will put your name on the mailbox. Before long, your actions will become second nature and this will be your norm. You won't have to put effort into taking pride in yourself, because you will be full of pride every day and in every action you take.

Self-check:
- ☐ Do I display pride in my work?
- ☐ Do I show pride in my unit?
- ☐ Do I have pride in my leadership role?
- ☐ Do my troops trust me to lead them?
- ☐ Do senior leaders trust me to lead my team?

Lesson Reminder

Become an expert at your current job

Staying in your lane is all about focusing your energy on the position or responsibility that you currently hold. The more you learn to stay in your lane, the better prepared you will be when promotions and other leadership opportunities come your way.

You may have to get out of your lane from time to time, and troops will understand. But when you do, make sure that you remain conscious of where you are. As your level of responsibility grows, you may be required to get outside of your lane more often. Be careful to ensure that you are working with subordinate leaders and leaders from other units when you get out of your lane.

If you are a senior NCO, senior officer, commander, or senior enlisted leader, your lane is pretty wide and you can move in and out as you need to ensure the entire unit is on track.

- What is the main point you took away from this lesson?

- How can you ensure you remain in your lane?

- How does the unit benefit when you stay in your lane?

- How does your team or unit benefit?

- What are the pitfalls of getting out of your lane?

- How do peers react when you get out of your lane?

List the items you will commit to in order to stay in your lane:

1)

2)

3)

When will I have these items complete?

Who will hold me accountable for these actions?

What are the consequences of not doing these items?

FINAL THOUGHTS:

Learning to stay in your lane will not hinder your progress. Senior leaders will respect you for the fact that you take your role seriously. Once you have proven yourself in that role, your supervisor or your commander will be ready to give you more.

Staying in your lane will help you grow professionally and aide you in avoiding failure. Those who move up too fast, often struggle to achieve goals at the next level. Be willing to accept staying in your lane until the unit needs you to do something else. Do everything you can to prepare for that when the time is right.

Self-check:
- ☐ Do I stay in my lane most of the time?
- ☐ Do others perceive me as staying in my lane?
- ☐ Do I know when I get out of my lane?
- ☐ Do I know the pitfalls of getting out of my lane?
- ☐ Do I still grow professionally in my lane?

Lesson Reminder

Make it your business to know them

The equipment guy lesson is a reminder that a leader needs to know their troops. There are equipment guys in every military unit. By knowing who the equipment guy is, you can spend time getting to know him and making sure he knows how important he is to your team's success. The equipment guy is always a critical member of your unit.

Leaders can get caught up in how important their function is, and forget to look around and take notice of the others working hard to support them. You should avoid this mentality, and always put proper time and attention on your subordinates.

Some leaders look for the privilege that is afforded them by their position. They want parking spots dedicated to them, or a seat at the head table during formal events. Troops see those actions and form the opinion that you care more about yourself than you do about them. Leaders who get this lesson will give up their seat at the head table when the time is right, and will offer their parking spot to others from time to time. They know that caring about the equipment guy pays huge dividends.

- What is the key point of this lesson?

- Who is your equipment guy?

- What are the benefits of knowing the equipment guy?

- How do troops feel when you spend time with them?

- How can you show appreciation for troops?

- How can you help the equipment guy grow and develop?

List the items you will commit to so you know the equipment guy:

1)

2)

3)

When will I have these items complete?

Who will hold me accountable for these actions?

What are the consequences of not doing these items?

FINAL THOUGHTS:

Get to know your troops and they will work harder than you can ever expect. Invest time and effort into getting to know them and you will earn their respect.

Be careful not to get too familiar with your troops as you get to know them. When they become too close to their leader, they may expect special treatment when they fail to perform. Others may also form perceptions of favoritism if you get too close to them. Perceptions are powerful and drive people to lose confidence in you as a leader. There has to be a hard line of distinction between being a leader and being their friend.

You can always be friendly while remaining professional in all situations. Don't let those lines get blurred.

Self-check:
- ☐ Do I spend time with the equipment guy?
- ☐ Do I know enough about each of them?
- ☐ Do I show them sincere appreciation?
- ☐ Do I help them grow professionally?
- ☐ Do I make them feel important?

Lesson Reminder

Everyone adds value to the mission

Just fix trucks is a lesson designed to help leaders relate the work the troop does to the mission of the unit. Troops need to know their job and the mission of the unit. More importantly, they must know how they add value to the overall success of the unit and your service.

As you grow in leadership responsibility and your span of control expands, you have to schedule time to get out to where the people fix your trucks and talk with them about how they contribute.

This is all about helping your troops see and understand the big picture. Take them from the tactical level to the strategic level in their thinking, just like the young man in this lesson did by understanding that fixing trucks helped put bombs on target.

- What was the key point of this lesson?

- How well do your troops know the mission?

- How well do troops understand their job?

- How can you help your troops relate their job to the overall mission?

- How well do your troops understand the goals of the company?

- What impact does this lesson have on morale?

List the items you will commit to so your people know how important they are to the mission:

1)

2)

3)

When will I have these items complete?

Who will hold me accountable for these actions?

What are the consequences of not doing these items?

FINAL THOUGHTS:

Don't be satisfied if your troops can recite your mission statement or have familiarity with your strategic goals. Knowing the words is just the start. They need to know what those words mean and they have to relate their duty to those words.

Your troops need to hear you talking about the mission statement and using those words with meaning. If you downplay understanding of the mission, they will begin to wonder why they need to know it when you do not.

Beyond the mission statement, most services have creeds. Troops need to know their creed, and they need to believe in their creed. Unfortunately some senior leaders, officer and NCO, do not know their own service creed, service song, or their mission statement. If you are a leader and cannot recite them in public, there is little chance that you can articulate them to the troops. Your credibility will take a huge hit.

Challenge your troops to relate what they are doing to the mission statement during every formation or meeting. This small way of holding them accountable for knowing the mission will pay dividends as they focus on what is important.

Self-check:

- ☐ Do I ensure troops know their job?
- ☐ Do I encourage them to be good at their job?
- ☐ Do I ensure troops know the mission?
- ☐ Do I help troops relate to the mission?
- ☐ Do I relate their importance to the mission?

Lesson Reminder

Experience what your troops do every day

Walk the mile is a lesson about getting out from behind your desk and spending time side by side with the troops so that you understand what they do every day. Placing yourself side by side with your troops is going to open you up to some great discussions and discoveries.

If you are a senior leader in the unit, there will be other leaders between you and the troops who are concerned about why you are doing this. Make sure they understand what you are doing, and assure them that you are not walking miles to check on them. However, if the subordinate leader is not doing his job, the troops will be sure to let you know. When you get feedback of this nature while walking the mile, do not become reactive. Take note, and after considering the factors presented and evaluating the situation, sit down and discuss the feedback with the leader in question.

Trust among leaders at all levels is important. Make sure that you do not lose the loyalty of subordinate level leaders because you always take the side of the troops based on what you hear while walking the mile with them. More likely, your observations of troop performance while walking the mile will give you a good indication of the effectiveness of leaders in charge of the troops.

- What is the main point of walking the mile?

- How do you interact with troops while on the mile?

- Are the troops responsive to you on the mile?

- How can you develop relationships while walking the mile?

- What can you learn from troops on the mile?

- What are the potential pitfalls of walking the mile?

List the items you will commit to in walking the mile with your people:

1)

2)

3)

When will I have these items complete?

Who will hold me accountable for these actions?

What are the consequences of not doing these items?

FINAL THOUGHTS:

Don't be fooled into thinking that everything you find while walking the mile will be positive. You may run across some bad practices or situations that require you to act promptly. Remember the word act means to do something. If you seem reactive, or if you over react, the result can even be worse.

Be calm, gather information, and make a decision about what to do. Know that the person with the best solution to the problem you discovered could be the troop you are walking the mile with. Ask them how they would do it differently or how they would fix the problem. They've been dealing with it routinely and maybe have spent hours trying to figure out a better way. Keeping your eyes and ears open here will pay great dividends.

Of course if the problem is safety related, you have to take immediate action to stop the practice. Just do it firmly without showing outward signs of stress.

Self-check:

- ☐ Do I spend time on the job with my troops?
- ☐ Do I add value to their job while on the mile?
- ☐ Do I dig in and ask questions about their job?
- ☐ Do I show genuine interest in their skills?
- ☐ Do I leave them energized?

Lesson Reminder

Show respect by meeting face to face

A cup of my coffee is the title chapter and even though it took place at the onset of email usage on personal computers, has relevancy today as more technology is being used by everyone in the military. No matter how much technology is used by the troops and your military unit, there is now and always will be, value in meeting with people face to face and showing them respect.

Imagine how good people feel when you take the time to stop what you are doing and meet with them before getting down to business. Never underestimate that power.

- Describe the main point of this lesson?

- List the benefits of face to face (F2F) meetings?

- What are the pitfalls of not meeting F2F?

- How much time are you willing to commit to F2F meetings?

- How do you know if the F2F meeting was effective?

- When/why is email effective in sending messages?

List the items you will commit to in meeting people face to face:

1)

2)

3)

When will I have these items complete?

Who will hold me accountable for these actions?

What are the consequences of not doing these items?

FINAL THOUGHTS:

The world of technology continues to move at light speed. Before long, most people will be out of the email business because it's too slow and too cumbersome. Texting will pass too, and communication through electronic means will change faster than the text of this book can. But one thing will always have a place in the military, and that is meeting people face to face.

Self-check:

- ☐ Do I make time for F2F meetings?
- ☐ Do I host other leaders for F2F meetings?
- ☐ Do I provide follow up after F2F meetings?
- ☐ Do I understand the value of showing respect?
- ☐ Do I understand how to use electronic communications?

Lesson Reminder

Provide honest and direct feedback

A good mirror is a lesson about giving honest and direct feedback to your troops. This feedback technique is best used when poor performance or inappropriate behavior has taken place. During situations like that, there is no need to have discussion, you just need to make the point. However, if you do this every time you sit down with your troops to provide feedback, they will be stressed out from the moment you schedule the meeting.

Like all feedback, you should follow up with the recipient after using this direct method. You have to ensure the message was clearly received and corrective actions were properly implemented. If the actions of the recipient are not in line with the expectations, then you may need to have additional feedback sessions that are less direct to allow for some discussion.

- What is the main point of this lesson?

- How does honest and direct feedback impact your troops?

- Why should you eliminate debate during honest and direct feedback?

- What are the potential pitfalls of honest and direct feedback?

- How can you become comfortable giving direct feedback?

- What is the best way to follow up on direct feedback?

List the items you will commit to so you provide a better mirror for your people:

1)

2)

3)

When will I have these items complete?

Who will hold me accountable for these actions?

What are the consequences of not doing these items?

FINAL THOUGHTS:

Always remember that giving honest and direct feedback is like making the troop look into a mirror and evaluate their actions. If you are worried about hurting the feelings of the person you are providing with honest and direct feedback, step back and realize that this is not personal. Remove emotions from this situation as much as possible.

This method of providing feedback is designed to help the troop be successful at what they are doing. If they cannot see that your effort is intended to help them, and they fail to make corrections to the performance or behavior, it may be time to consider other administrative actions.

Self-check:

- ☐ Do I provide honest and direct feedback?
- ☐ Do I encourage change based on my feedback?
- ☐ Do I ensure feedback does not become personal?
- ☐ Do I accept feedback on my performance?
- ☐ Do I make changes based on feedback received?

Lesson Reminder

Leave it better than you found it

Improving the foxhole is a lesson about challenging the status quo and being innovative. As a leader you have to lead troops in challenging the status quo and looking for new and improved ways of handling mission objectives. You also have to encourage your troops to do the same. Military units should be constantly focused on finding new ways to attack mission objectives.

Small teams within military units find it easier to change through innovation. It's much tougher for the military services to change, they are so large and complex, and it's difficult to implement wide-scale changes. But when the military service directs a change in the way operations are to be conducted, leaders at all levels need to get on board and implement that change. Leaders have to be creative and encourage creative behavior by their teams. Troops will follow your lead on innovation because they generally like to contribute to the mission.

- What did you get out of this lesson?

- How do you challenge the status quo as a leader?

- How do troops challenge the status quo?

- How do you create an environment of innovation?

- How do you help troops understand change?

- How do you respond to complaints about change?

List the items you will commit to so you can improve your foxhole:

1)

2)

3)

When will I have these items complete?

Who will hold me accountable for these actions?

What are the consequences of not doing these items?

FINAL THOUGHTS:

Everyone is counting on you to lead change. They want to know that it is OK to think about new ideas and concepts and that you will be supportive of them. Your willingness to lead change will have a highly positive impact on the success of the unit.

Conversely, your unwillingness to accept change, manage change, and incorporate change into your operations will likely lead to your failure. Don't be the reason your team is left behind.

Self-check:

- ☐ Do I think innovatively?
- ☐ Do I encourage challenges to the status quo?
- ☐ Do I help troops understand change?
- ☐ Do I handle complaints about change?
- ☐ Do leave things better for the next person?

Lesson Reminder

Always consider exceptions to policy

The leadership line lesson is about knowing the written rules before making a decision, but understanding the exceptions to policy and how they apply. Not every situation that a leader could face will include exceptions to policy, so use this one as needed when things are not neatly presented on the line.

Confident leaders understand the difference between making normal decisions and being able to decide on things that fall outside the lines. You have to be willing to act when things are not clear, taking risk and remaining accountable for your actions.

- What did you learn from this lesson?

- How do your leadership decisions impact the mission?

- How are you perceived as a decision maker?

- How do troops respond to your leadership decisions?

- How do you handle criticism of your leadership decisions?

- What factors must be considered outside the line?

List the items you will commit to in making decisions off the leadership line:

1)

2)

3)

When will I have these items complete?

Who will hold me accountable for these actions?

What are the consequences of not doing these items?

FINAL THOUGHTS:

There are few easy days as a military leader. When the tough days happen, you have to be ready and able. Using this lesson to help guide you will be beneficial because even the tough days are not scripted. Every leadership situation will be different and will require your full attention to get it right.

Those who fail to stay attuned to the exceptions to policy and work only on the line could lose the support of the troops who work for them.

Self-check:
- ☐ Do I know and understand the leadership line?
- ☐ Do I make sound and informed decisions?
- ☐ Do I understand the exceptions to policy?
- ☐ Do I understand consequences of my decisions?
- ☐ Do I stand behind the decisions I make?

Lesson Reminder

Make decisions during difficult times

The courageous leadership lesson is provided to help leaders make tough decisions during difficult times. Imagine that your decisions could lead to the success or failure of the operation. This is certainly possible for any leader, and comes with a high price for failure. Your decisions will impact careers and even lives. Potentially what you decide will ultimately lead to the best outcome for everyone involved.

Courage does not come naturally. You may have to work hard to develop the courage to make tough decisions. People will respect that you are making sure you make the decision which is best for the team and not just the easy one that would be the most popular.

- What is the key take away from this lesson?

- How can your decisions impact your troops?

- How can you display confidence in your decision?

- How do troops react to courageous decisions?

- How do troops relate to tough decision makers?

- How do troops react to risk adverse leaders?

List the items you will commit to in making tough decisions:

1)

2)

3)

When will I have these items complete?

Who will hold me accountable for these actions?

What are the consequences of not doing these items?

FINAL THOUGHTS:

Making good, sound decisions is essential for success. But it will not always be easy. There are many things you have to consider, and the outcome of your decision could have a major impact on your unit and the troops. Making a poor decision as a leader will negatively impact your unit.

If you really want your earn the respect of your troops, be ready to make the tough decisions, regardless of how unpopular they are.

Self-check:
- ☐ Am I prepared to make tough decisions?
- ☐ Do I have confidence in my decisions?
- ☐ Do I control my emotions during difficult times?
- ☐ Do I have the courage to make the right decision?
- ☐ Do I explain my decisions when times permits?

ABOUT THE AUTHOR

Scott H. Dearduff retired from the United States Air Force in January 2011 following more than 29 years of active duty service. At the culmination of his career he served as the Command Chief Master Sergeant for Ninth Air Force and United States Air Forces Central Command. He amassed more than 1000 days deployed to combat operations in the Central Command Area of Operations. Prior to his combat deployments in Iraq and Afghanistan, he served in more than 20 countries around the world and has traveled to more than 50 foreign countries. His leadership skills were honed under fire during nuclear security operations, Presidential security, disaster relief operations, humanitarian relief, aircraft accidents and an active shooter response with mass casualties. Along the way he obtained a Bachelor's Degree in Management and a double minor in Criminal Justice and Business Management. His military decorations include the Legion of Merit, 3 Bronze Star Medals, Afghanistan and Iraq Campaign Medals with multiple service stars, and the Air Force Combat Action Medal among more than 27 total decorations. He is the recipient of the James M. Shamess Award for Literary Excellence and was named a Distinguished Alumni from Spruce Creek High School in Florida.

You may contact the Chief at dearduffconsulting@gmail.com

Other books available:
Chief, My Journey Thru Iraq at the Peak of War
A Cup of My Coffee, Lessons for Life
A Cup of My Coffee 2, Military Lessons for Business leaders